Soccer
Great Moments, Records, and Facts

by Teddy Borth

ABDO
GREAT SPORTS
Kids

abdopublishing.com

Published by Abdo Kids, a division of ABDO, PO Box 398166, Minneapolis, Minnesota 55439.

Copyright © 2015 by Abdo Consulting Group, Inc. International copyrights reserved in all countries. No part of this book may be reproduced in any form without written permission from the publisher.

Printed in the United States of America, North Mankato, Minnesota.

102014

012015

Photo Credits: AP Images, Corbis, iStock, Shutterstock, © Natursports p.7, © AGIF p.11 / Shutterstock.com

Production Contributors: Teddy Borth, Jennie Forsberg, Grace Hansen

Design Contributors: Laura Rask, Dorothy Toth

Library of Congress Control Number: 2014943664

Cataloging-in-Publication Data

Borth, Teddy.

 Soccer : great moments, records, and facts / Teddy Borth.

   p. cm. -- (Great sports)

ISBN 978-1-62970-692-4 (lib. bdg.)

Includes bibliographical references and index.

1. Soccer--Juvenile literature.   I. Title.

796.334--dc23

                2014943664

Table of Contents

Soccer

Early soccer was played in China. It was around 200 bc. The net was tied to bamboo. Today's soccer started in 1863.

The Field

The field is also called the pitch. Every country in the world has soccer fields.

Great Records

Pelé is from **Brazil**. He is one of the best of all time. He won 3 **World Cups**. That is the most for one player.

Brazil

Lionel Messi is from **Argentina**.

He won "player of the year"

4 times in a row.

Argentina

11

Steaua Bucuresti is a team in **Romania**. From 1986 to 1989 they never lost. That is 119 games in a row!

Romania

13

Cheers for Number 19

Stiliyan Petrov played for

Aston Villa. He was the captain.

In 2012 he learned he had

cancer. He had to stop playing.

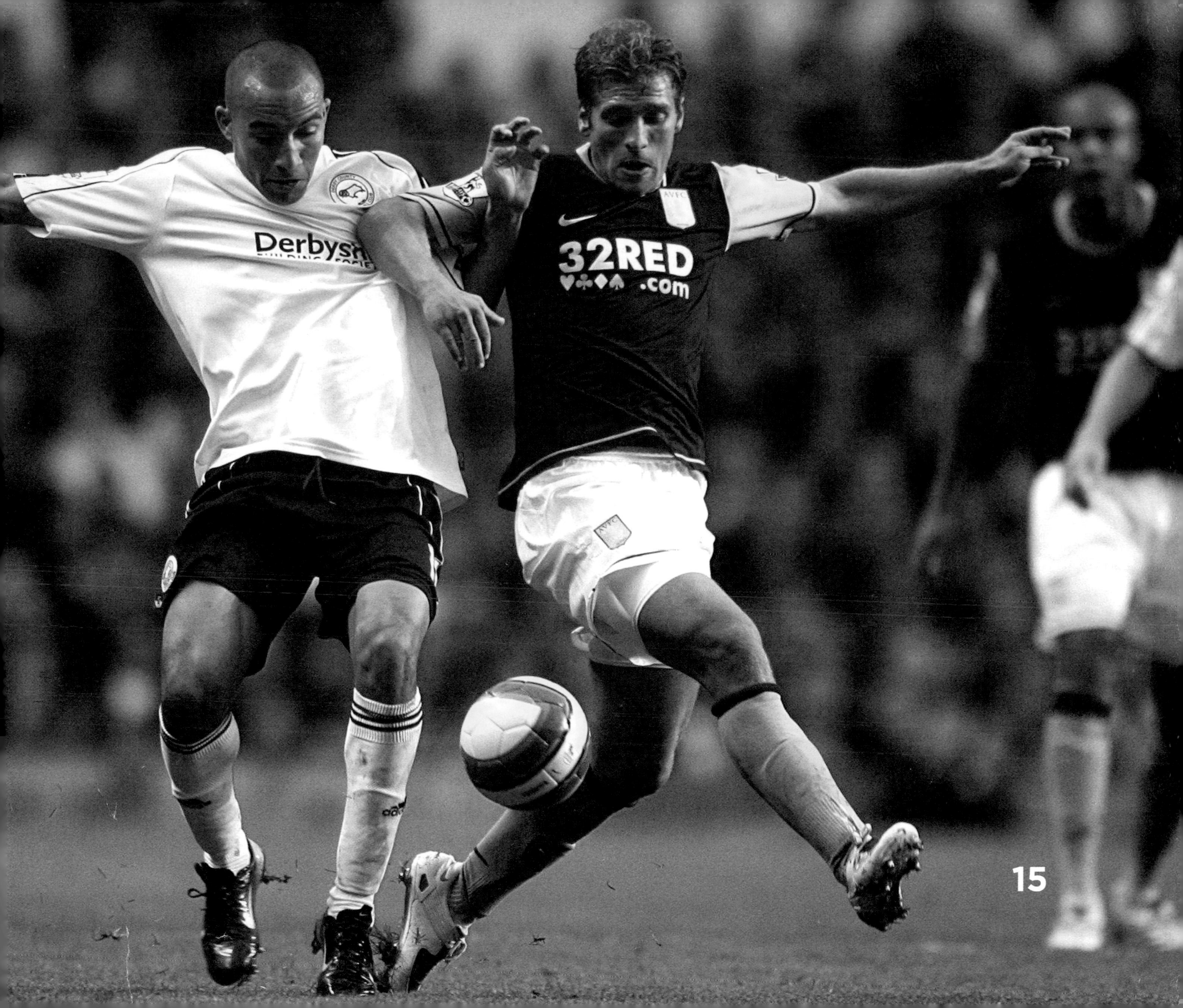
Derbysh
32RED
.com

He went to watch a game. The fans cheered at the 19-minute mark. They were cheering for him. His **jersey** number was 19. Fans still cheer for him at games.

The Rise of Cameroon

Cameroon is a country in Africa. Its soccer team played in the 1990 **World Cup**. Nobody thought it would go far.

Cameroon

19

Cameroon shocked everyone. It beat 3 teams. It was one of the final 8 teams. That is a first for an African team. It put Africa on the soccer map.

More Facts

- Soccer players run about 7 miles (11 km) during a game.

- There are over 250 million soccer players in the world. More than 3.5 billion people are soccer fans.

- Martinho Orige of **Brazil** juggled a soccer ball nonstop for 19 hours and 30 minutes! He kept the ball in the air using only his feet, legs, and head.

Glossary

Argentina – a country in South America.

Aston Villa – a soccer team in England. It is one of the oldest teams. It was formed in 1874.

Brazil – a country in South America.

cancer – a serious illness. Unhealthy cells grow in the body, causing sickness.

jersey – the uniform a player wears. It can have the player's name and number on it.

Romania – a country in Europe.

World Cup – an event where soccer teams around the world play each other. It is held every four years.

Index

abdokids.com

Use this code to log on to abdokids.com and access crafts, games, videos, and more!

Abdo Kids Code:
GSK6924